From America to Africa

 THREE SIBLINGS JOURNEY 

Published by Spines
ISBN: 979-8-89383-619-6

From America to Africa

 THREE SIBLINGS JOURNEY 

Davin, Rhema, and Noah

On a hot day in the Ivory Coast, three young siblings gathered around their living room with a few friends and shared stories about their big move from America to Africa.

Davin began, "We lived in a small town called High Point in North Carolina." Davin recalled. "I shared a bedroom with my big brother, Justin, and my little brother, Noah. It was the boys' room."

Rhema smiled, "I had a room all to myself, with a desk, a tent and toys!"

'Oh," Noah said. "I was too young. I don't even remember America."

Davin continued, "We went to a Christian school, where we learned about the Bible."

Noah
Rhema
Kendra
Davin
Amir

"Our parents talked about going to Africa a lot," Rhema explained, "since they're originally from there.

" One random school day, we came back home, and to our surprise, we found our parents packing our stuff!"

"We couldn't figure out what was going on. So, I asked. Mommy, why are you packing our stuff?" Davin said.

Mom reminded us, "Well, we're going to Africa. Remember we talked about it before?"

"Oh yeah!" Davin said.

Rhema shared, "Mom said I was so excited. I had been to Africa before. Unfortunately, I didn't remember because I was a baby."

Davin said, "I remembered my time in Africa."

Noah sighed, "I had never been to Africa because I wasn't born."

"Then Mom took me shopping to buy little gifts for my friends before our last day of school. I knew that the next day would be my last day at school, because Mom had already informed our teachers that we would be moving to Africa in the coming days," Rhema said.

"Me, too," and "Me, three!" Davin and Noah shouted.

"After that day, I went into my room, but....MY BED. WHERE IS IT?" Rhema shared.

Davin laughed, "My bed was gone, too. Our parents had packed everything."

Rhema added, "That night, we slept in my bedless room."

"Oh, wow! What did you do with all your stuff? Amir, one of their friends, asked.

"We had to give away stuff and sell some because we couldn't fit everything in a container," Davin explained. Our aunts and my uncle came to our house to help us pack the remaining stuff and throw away what we didn't need. We also gave away some stuff.

"After the house was emptied and cleaned, we prayed for a safe trip. Then we gathered our luggage and left, saying goodbye to our house and everyone for the last time." Davin shared, with a quiver in his voice.

"And then we said goodbye to our house and everyone," Rhema added sadly.

Kendra added, "Oh, no, that must have been so hard to do."

"And we flew to Africa in two flights," Rhema continued. "We watched movies and ate food that looked weird but tasted good. It was a long trip, and we were sooo tired!

" Our ears were hurting, and Noah cried a lot. But finally, we arrived in Abidjan, Ivory Coast," Davin explained.

 "You must have been so happy to finally get here," said Amir.

"Yes. We first stayed at our aunt's house before we got to our house. This place is wonderful," Rhema shared.

"What else was it like when you first arrived?" asked Kendra.

"We were home-schooled, which was quite boring, but it ended quickly and, I had fun playing with my cousin, Yoan, and everyone else," said Davin.

"Me too!" and "Me, three!" yelled Rhema and Noah.

Davin said, "Well, we've been here for quite some time now and I love it here. The food is delicious, and my friends are wonderful. My favorite local foods are Alloco, fried plantain) and Garba, Atieke with fish and little bit of onions.

"I am eating good food. My favorite local foods are Garba, Alloco and plantain chips." Rhema added.

"I love Alloco", said Noah

Davin shared, "I learned a lot of French because everyone in the Ivory Coast speaks French. But I am still learning."

"Me too," Rhema gushed.

Noah cheered, "Oui, oui!"

"Anyhoo, I even learned how to play soccer, they call it football here, and I also learned a little bit of basketball, and I still am learning," Davin grinned.

"And I also learned a whole lot of soccer. They even call me "Lady Drogba" a famous soccer player from the Ivory Coast," chimed in Rhema. "I miss my aunts, uncles, and cousins in America. I miss my house and eating McDonald's. But I have a nice school with nice friends, and love it here. Ivory Coast is a very wonderful place and I have a good life here."

"Me, too," and "Me, three!" Davin and Noah shouted.

The End